STEP CLOSER

A SIX WEEK DEVOTIONAL
AND GROUP STUDY GUIDE

DR. NATE RUCH

STEP CLOSER

Small Group Study Guide
Edition 1.1
Copyright © 2018 Emmanuel

Requests for information should be addressed to:
Emmanuel
7777 University Ave. NE
Spring Lake Park, MN 55432

ISBN-13: 978-1723033766
ISBN-10: 1723033766

TABLE OF CONTENTS

CONTENTS

Acknowledgments 1

#Stepcloser (Introduction) 2

Week One: How do I step closer to God when I'm overlooked? 5

Week Two: How do I step closer to God when I'm facing a giant? 25

Week Three: How do I step closer to God when I'm dodging spears? 45

Week Four: How do I step closer to God when my dream is gone? 65

Week Five: How do I step closer to God in the middle of a mess? 85

Week Six: How do I step closer to God when my dream comes true? 105

Conclusion 125

Small Group Resources 126

ACKNOWLEDGMENTS

Thank you to Christine Hofler, Rachel Jordahl, Andrew Mason, Lenny Ouradnik, Becky Meyerson, Justin Petrick and Kevin Senapatiratne for their inspiring and heartfelt writing contributions to this resource. Thank you to Laura Wegener for her editing skills on this project. Thank you to our staff team members Bri Cordle, Andrew Baccam and Mattie Kidder for their excellence on the overall design and format. Thank you to Pastors Mark Alan Schoolmeesters, JonCarlos Velez and our Emmanuel Worship and Production team for their anointed efforts on the incredible worship videos that work with this study guide. Thank you to Stephen Konsor for his filming and editing on the teaching videos and Art Hooker for his efforts on the filming and editing of the worship videos. And last, but definitely not least, thank you to my wonderful wife, Jodi Ruch, for her powerful; teaching in the video series as well. This would not have been possible without all of you!

#STEPCLOSER

Life is a battle. We battle for godly relationships. We long for financial stability. We hope for fulfillment, both on the outside and on the inside. Circumstances wage war against us, and at times, people push us away.

But we don't need to be overwhelmed by what goes on around us. We can employ the God-given secret weapon James talks about in James 4:8.

"COME CLOSE TO GOD, AND GOD WILL COME CLOSE TO YOU"

Step closer. This two-word weapon helps us resist the enemy of our soul. This weapon helps us manage the obstacles the enemy puts in our way to dissuade us from pursuing Jesus.

One person in the Bible stands out as an example of what this weapon looks like in action: David. Most people recognize him as the shepherd boy who slayed a giant, but that's only a portion of his story. He authored over half of the book of Psalms, ran for his life from the king of Israel before eventually becoming the new king of Israel.

David's achievements are so well known, it's easy to view him as a fabled figure. Take a closer look at his story, however, and you'll see a flawed indvidual who endured personal struggles and intense levels of external opposition from the people around him.

His weapon to sidestepping the traps of the enemy and living life well is the same one you have today. As we take a fresh look into his life, let's arm ourselves with the same secret weapon: stepping closer to God.

HOW TO GET THE MOST OUT OF THIS STUDY GUIDE:

Here is a brief explanation of the features of this study guide.

- **Group curriculum** that allows you to follow along for each group discussion. The curriculum works alongside the Step Closer video series. The video series is 6 group sessions that each include a teaching video to get the group discussion going as well as worship video content to use for the closing prayer time.
- **Scripture Memory** verses for each week.
- **A 42-day devotional** for daily reading and inspiration. Each devotional includes a short prayer to launch your prayer time for the day.
- **Personal Reflection** is a Designated space for daily journal entries.
- **Praise and Worship vocabulary** list in the back of the book to help you grow in your verbal expression of praise and worship.
- **Resources** in the back of the book for hosting your own Step Closer Group

SESSION 1:
HOW DO I STEP CLOSER TO GOD WHEN I'M OVERLOOKED?

SCRIPTURE MEMORY

"But I, the LORD, search all hearts and examine secret motives. I give all people their due rewards, according to what their actions deserve."
– Jeremiah 17:10, NLT

WELCOME

Each week, give people 5-10 minutes to find your location and arrive. If possible, provide light snacks and have upbeat Christian music playing in the background until you officially begin your group meeting.

CHECKING IN

INTRO: If this is your group's first meeting or if you have new group members, be sure to introduce yourselves and have others introduce themselves as well. Review the Small Group Guidelines on page 127 of this study guide.

ASK: If you could swap roles with someone for a day, whom would you choose?

 **WATCH: PLAY SESSION 1A OF THE STEP CLOSER VIDEO SERIES AND TAKE NOTES ON THE PAGE PROVIDED.**

GROUP DISCUSSION QUESTIONS

#1 HAVE SOMEONE READ OUT LOUD: 1 Samuel 16:1-13

>**READ OUT LOUD:** In the video, we learn that Jesse had all his sons, except David, brought before Samuel.

>**ASK:** What emotions could David have experienced from not initially being invited by his father to the sacrifice with Samuel?

#2 HAVE SOMEONE READ OUT LOUD: 1 Samuel 16:7

>**READ OUT LOUD:** Even though David was overlooked by man, he was not being overlooked by God. In fact, it was the way David handled moments of being overlooked by people that attracted the attention of God to his life the most.

>**ASK:** What can this teach us about the nature of God towards a person when no one else is paying attention to them?

#3 READ OUT LOUD: There are times in everyone's life where we experience being overlooked.

>**ASK:** When were you overlooked for something but later in life realized that being overlooked ended up being a blessing?

#4 HAVE SOMEONE READ OUT LOUD: 1 Samuel 16:14-23

>**READ OUT LOUD:** David has been anointed as the next king, however we read next that he isn't called to a throne but to serve the one currently on it, Saul.

>**ASK:** Have you served under a person who took the position or attention you thought that you deserved? What was the posture of your attitude while serving?

#5 READ THE FOLLOWING PASSAGE OUT LOUD:

"I will not forget you! See, I have engraved you on the
palms of my hands."

- Isaiah 49:15b-16a NIV

READ OUT LOUD: God has not overlooked or forgotten
you, in fact you matter so much to Him that He lovingly
looks at those scars on His hands. During years of being
overlooked, David surrendered to the truth that God loved
him and had a plan for his life. God has a plan for your
life too. You have NEVER been overlooked, no matter the
circumstance. We learn from the life of David that
surrender was essential to his relationship with God.

ASK: Is there anything in your life that you need to
surrender to God to move closer to Him?

WORSHIP AND PRAYER TIME

PRAYER REQUESTS: Ask for everyone's prayer requests. Encourage everyone to briefly share their requests so you can spend more time praying for your requests than talking about them. Be sure to record them on the Small Group Prayer and Praise Report on pages 130 - 131 of this study guide. Commit to pray for each other's requests every day this week. Once all the requests are gathered, move into a group prayer time.

GROUP WORSHIP TIME:

 Before you pray for each other, invite the Presence of the Lord into your time by playing the worship video for this week (Session 1B). As the worship time concludes flow into your time of prayer by praying over the prayer requests. Encourage the group to participate by praying for one of the prayer requests that were given.

WORSHIP OPTION/ACTIVITY: If you're meeting online, in a café or in a setting that is not conducive for playing the worship video, use the following worship exercise before moving into prayer...

- Have someone read out loud the worshipful Psalm of Psalm 139:1-18 or assign each person to read 3-6 verses each, depending on how many people are there. (ex: 6 people could each read 3 verses, or 3 people could each read 6 verses).
- After reading it out loud, have a minute of silence to each write down any one or two of the verses in your own words on the next page. Use the verse(s) that touched you or stood out to you the most.
- Then, have each person pray what they wrote out back to God in the group.
- Take 10-15 seconds to wait on God and His Presence before starting to pray for each other.

_____

_____

_____

_____

_____

_____

_____

_____

_____

_____

PRAYER: If praying in a group is new or uncomfortable for you, we encourage you to start by praying single-sentence prayers. Don't worry about how fancy you sound. God isn't looking for eloquence. He just wants honesty. Talk to God like you talk to a friend. Give everyone a chance to pray, but don't insist on it. Over time, you will all feel much more comfortable praying together.

DISMISSAL

- Remind everyone about the next group meeting.
- Encourage everyone to continue to pray for each other throughout the week.
- Encourage group members to invite anybody they think will benefit from being in the group to the next meeting.
- Collect basic contact information such as phone numbers and email addresses for your group members. The Small Group Roster on page 129 of this study guide is a good place to record this information.

Ignite the ultimate chain reaction.

Today's Scripture: Acts 13:22

God wants to be in a relationship with you. The Creator of the Universe, Who holds the galaxies and space itself in the palm of His hand, wants to talk to you on a daily basis.

But He is a gentleman, and He will only be a part of your life if you invite Him in.

This is an invitation for all men and women. James 4:8 tells us what that invitation to God looks like:

> ## *"Come close to God, and God will come close to you."*

In other words, as we step closer to God, He will step closer to us. By faith, we take a step toward God in our thoughts, words, attitudes, and actions. Every time we do so, we invite God to move in our lives—and God's promise is that He will step closer to us in return.

David lived this out. That's why the Bible tells us he was a man after God's own heart. Through every situation he faced in life, he always kept moving toward heaven... and we should too. Let's learn together how we can follow his pattern of living to step closer.

PRAYER: Lord, thank You for Your promise to step closer to me as I take a step towards You. Show me how I can take one step closer to You today. In Jesus' name, amen.

NOTES

Identify our common enemy.

Today's Scripture: John 10:10

We have a common enemy. He seeks to derail us from stepping closer to God. The enemy of our soul wants every step toward heaven to be followed by 2-3 steps back.

We must be aware that the enemy will deploy obstacles and circumstances to dissuade us from pursuing Jesus. His tactics differ for each person and in different seasons of life, but his goal remains the same: to steal, kill and destroy our faith in God.

When you feel overlooked and you feel inferior, know the enemy is working overtime to skew your perspective toward his deception. The way we combat his strategies is through stepping closer to the Father.

Let's learn from David. He freely worshipped God in the fields with his sheep because he understood the principle found in James 4:7:

"So humble yourselves before God. Resist the devil, and he will flee from you."

Humility sets us up to resist the enemy and take step after step toward our Savior.

PRAYER: Lord, I humble myself before you. Because of Your power backing me up, I resist the enemy and he must flee.
In Jesus' name, amen.

NOTES

Imagine your potential.

Today's Scripture: 1 Samuel 16:1-13

If David's dad, Jesse, had his way, we wouldn't be talking about King David. We would be talking about King Eliab or King Abinadab. In fact, any of the seven sons he brought to the prophet Samuel seemed like they would be a good option to become king. That's why Jesse left David in the fields to tend sheep.

He didn't think David could be Israel's new king—but God did.

The moment David realized he wasn't included in his dad's first pick to show Samuel had to have hurt. But he didn't let that exclusion foster rejection or create resentment. He knew he was under the watchful eye of the person who mattered most: Almighty God.

No matter what's going on in your life today, know that God sees you. Other people may not see your talent or your potential, but God does. He will exalt you as you humbly step toward Him... again and again and again.

PRAYER: Lord, thank You for caring about me. I trust that You will finish the good work You have begun in my life. In Jesus' name, amen.

NOTES

Increase your time with God.

Today's Scripture: 1 Samuel 16:6-7

When Samuel first saw Eliab, he actually agreed with Jesse. In 1 Samuel 16:6, Samuel "took one look at Eliab and thought, 'Surely this is the Lord's anointed!'"

The Lord's response to Samuel is key:

> *"...Don't judge by his appearance or height, for I have rejected him. The Lord doesn't see things the way you see them. People judge by outward appearance, but the Lord looks at the heart."*

1 Samuel 16:7

Outward appearances can be deceiving. When that's all we rely on, we will always be disappointed. We need to look at each other—and ourselves—fully aware that there's more to each of our stories than what people see.

What we don't see, God does see. He watched David faithfully protect his sheep from wild animals. He saw David spending time playing his harp when the sheep were his only audience. God knew David's full story.

Being overlooked by people can feel devastating, but it is momentary. God responds to what we cultivate in the quiet spaces of life. He sees the heart, and that's what truly counts.

PRAYER: Lord, help me not to focus on my public perception; rather, help me to be faithful to You when no one else is watching. In Jesus' name, amen.

NOTES

Instill patience in your plan.

Today's Scripture: 1 Samuel 16:12-13

When Samuel left Jesse's house after he had anointed David as king, David was left in an unusual position. He has just been elevated above the rest of his family to eventually become the highest position of authority in the land. The conversation around the dinner table that night must have been interesting!

David had a choice to make as that day finished and a crown wasn't immediately placed on his head. In fact, he had weeks, months, and years that followed without any sign it would become true.

Should he try to make it happen?

Certainly not. Any time we take charge of making God's plans come true, we tread on dangerous ground. David made a decision to let King Saul reign, despite the fact he knew he would be the next king. As we'll see more and more over the next few weeks, David wouldn't touch the Lord's anointed—and neither should you.

The direction God gives you won't always come true as you plan. Be patient. The people who made you feel inferior will be able to watch God exalt you in due time.

PRAYER: Lord, thank You that I don't have to make Your plan happen. All I have to do is follow your direction. Help me to be patient in the process. In Jesus' name, amen.

NOTES

Initiate the power of worship.

Today's Scripture: 1 Samuel 16: 14-23

David's days of being a shepherd gave him plenty of time to create a powerful pattern of worship in his life. He consistently moved closer to heaven, and eventually his efforts were seen by others. This is how one of Saul's servants described David:

> *"...One of Jesse's sons from Bethlehem is a talented harp player. Not only that—he is a brave warrior, a man of war, and has good judgment. He is also a fine-looking young man, and the Lord is with him."*
>
> **1 Samuel 16:18**

David's harp playing was exactly what the king needed at that time, so David was invited to play his harp for King Saul. Every time David worshipped at the palace, Saul's tormenting spirit left.

David didn't allow inferiority to stay in his thoughts. He didn't need people's approval; he knew God approved of him. As a result, new doors were opened for him.

In the same way, your worship of God will cultivate trust in Him. That trust will invite God's favor into your life, not because you want to be seen by others, but because you know you are already seen by God.

PRAYER: Lord, help me to develop intimacy with You on a daily basis. Prepare my heart for things you have in store for me.
In Jesus name, amen.

NOTES

Intimidate inferiority.

Today's Scripture: 1 Samuel 17:17-31

In 1 Samuel 17, David brought his brothers food while they were with the Israelite army fighting against the Philistines. While there, he heard Goliath taunting the Israelites—yet nobody responded. In fact, many Israelites just ran away!

David responded differently. He knew Goliath was messing with Almighty God and His people—and that wasn't right. He knew God could obliterate Goliath. He just wanted a vessel through whom to work. So David started to ask around, "Who is this pagan Philistine anyway, that he is allowed to defy the armies of the living God?" (verse 26).

This response annoyed David's brother. Listen to Eliab's words:

> ### "What are you doing around here anyway? ... What about those few sheep you're supposed to be taking care of?"
>
> **1 Samuel 17:28**

Eliab still didn't see what God saw in David, but it didn't matter. David fully intended to do something about this Philistine who was out to harm God's people.

Intimacy with God breaks intimidation before others.

PRAYER: Lord, develop spiritual muscle in my life to help me push back against the pain of being overlooked. Give me the disposition of David as I follow you. In Jesus' name, amen.

NOTES

SESSION 2:
HOW DO I STEP CLOSER TO GOD WHEN I'M FACING A GIANT?

SCRIPTURE MEMORY:

"For God has not given us a spirit of fear and timidity, but of power, love, and self-discipline."

– 2 Timothy 1:7, NLT

WELCOME

Each week, give people 5-10 minutes to find your location and arrive. If possible, provide light snacks and have upbeat Christian music playing in the background until you officially begin your group meeting.

CHECKING IN

ASK: What were you afraid of as a child growing up?

 **WATCH: PLAY SESSION 2A OF THE STEP CLOSER VIDEO SERIES AND TAKE NOTES ON THE PAGE PROVIDED.**

GROUP DISCUSSION QUESTIONS

#1 HAVE SOMEONE READ OUT LOUD: 1 Samuel 17:23-24

> **READ OUT LOUD:** Confronting Goliath not only moved David closer to his destiny, it also moved him closer to God.

> **ASK:** What would've happened if David reacted in fear to Goliath like the army of Israel did? Would that fear have moved David closer or further from God in his heart? Explain.

#2 HAVE SOMEONE READ OUT LOUD: 1 Samuel 17:34-37

> **READ OUT LOUD:** Before David even begins a battle with Goliath he speaks of victory; not his own victory, but the Lord's victory!

> **ASK:** Have you experienced a time when you clung to a promise that God gave you before it came to pass?

#3 READ OUT LOUD: 1 Samuel 17:45-47

> **READ OUT LOUD:** As David faces his giant, he declares several spiritual realities in this passage (ex: "I come to you in the name of the Lord" or "the Lord will deliver you into my hand," etc).

> **ASK:** Which one stands out and what does it reveal to us about David's faith.

#4 READ OUT LOUD: In the video, Dr. Nate said, "David came with a confidence from his private worship."

> **ASK:** How does stepping closer to God in worship help us to face our giants?

#5 READ OUT LOUD: 1 Samuel 17:48 (NLT) – "As Goliath moved closer to attack, David quickly ran to meet him". David didn't shy away from the giant that faced him; in fact he picked up the pace and ran right toward it.

> **ASK:** Is there a giant in your life that you are running towards and battling right now... or is there a giant in your life that you are fearfully running from right now? Explain.

#6 READ OUT LOUD: At the end of verse 47 it says "This is the Lord's battle, and he will give you to us!" David stood in victory before the stone was ever put in the sling. The time that David took to worship and seek God prepared him for this very moment.

> **ASK:** Are you making time to worship God as you face your giant(s)? If not, how can you start and what does adding worship to your daily life look like?

WORSHIP AND PRAYER TIME

PRAYER REQUESTS: Ask for everyone's prayer requests. Encourage everyone to briefly share their requests so you can spend more time praying for your requests than talking about them. Be sure to record them on the Small Group Prayer and Praise Report on pages 130-131 of this study guide. Commit to pray for each other's requests every day this week. Once all the requests are gathered, move into a group prayer time.

GROUP WORSHIP TIME:

Before you pray for each other, invite the Presence of the Lord into your time by playing the worship video for this week (Session 2B). As the worship time concludes flow into your time of prayer by praying over the prayer requests. Encourage the group to participate by praying for one of the prayer requests that were given.

WORSHIP OPTION/ACTIVITY: If you're meeting online, in a café or in a setting that is not conducive for playing the worship video, use the following worship exercise before moving into prayer...

- Think about where you have seen God at work in recent days and weeks? (Ex: something happened at work or a conversation with your spouse, etc)
- Take a moment and recognize that God was there in your midst and thank Him for being there and being here in this moment.
- Write it down on the next page.
- Turn it into a prayer with the group as an offering of worship.
- Once everyone has prayed their offering of worship, have a moment of silence (10-15 seconds) before you start to pray for each other's prayer requests.

_____

_____

_____

_____

_____

_____

_____

_____

_____

_____

PRAYER: If praying in a group is new or uncomfortable for you, we encourage you to start by praying single-sentence prayers. Don't worry about how fancy you sound. God isn't looking for eloquence. He just wants honesty. Talk to God like you talk to a friend. Give everyone a chance to pray, but don't insist on it. Over time, you will all feel much more comfortable praying together.

DISMISSAL

- Remind everyone about the next group meeting.
- Encourage everyone to continue to pray for each other throughout the week.
- Encourage group members to invite anybody they think will benefit from being in the group to the next meeting.
- Collect basic contact information such as phone numbers and email addresses for your group members. The Small Group Roster on page 129 of this study guide is a good place to record this information.
- **Worship Activity for Next Week:** If your group uses the worship activity instead of the worship videos prepare for next week in this way: Each person bring a short passage of scripture that is worshipful. You want it to be around 3-5 verses, but not much longer. More direction will be given next week.

Step toward faith.

Today's Scripture: 1 Samuel 17:32-37

A literal giant couldn't take David away from God's presence. He could have run away in fear from Goliath—much of Israel's army did! But David knew how to let faith rule. He had practiced stepping closer to God so often that in the middle of his greatest challenge to that point, he offered these words to Goliath:

> *"...You come to me with sword, spear, and javelin, but I come to you in the name of the Lord of Heaven's Armies..."*
>
> **1 Samuel 17:45**

David didn't leave God's presence when he went to fight his giant. He brought God with him.

If you're facing a fear-filled situation, it's natural to be afraid. Just don't stay there. Fear left to fester becomes unbelief of God's Word, His promises, and His abilities.

The key to facing giant circumstances is your focus. When we focus on the giant, we focus on fear. When we keep our eyes on God, we focus on faith—and fear leaves.

PRAYER: Lord, thank you that I don't have to face giants alone. Help me to always step toward faith and away from fear.
In Jesus' name, amen.

NOTES

Step toward God's ability.

Today's Scripture: 1 Samuel 17:22-26, 37

Goliath was physically intimidating to the Israeli army. Every time they looked at him, they ran. They knew Goliath would beat anyone in a one-on-one encounter, simply because of his size. They were intimidated into silence.

David, on the other hand, knew that his size wasn't what mattered. He had a bigger power backing him up.

Just as David could be confident before a nine-foot giant, we can be confident before negative circumstances. As the apostle Paul tells us in Romans 8:37, "overwhelming victory is ours through Christ, who loved us." We don't need to view giants through the lens of our ability to overcome them. We can view giants based on God's ability manifest through us.

Of course, your circumstances will never agree with you. They'll run their mouth as long as you'll let them. Just know that giants don't have the last say. God's love and ability is greater than every giant we face. His ability working through us will bring giants to the ground.

PRAYER: Lord, thank You for empowering me to fight giants. I purpose to walk with Your ability in mind, knowing Your love and power is greater than what I face. In Jesus' name, amen.

NOTES

Step away from pity.

Today's Scripture: 1 Samuel 17:34-37

When wild animals attacked David's sheep, David had two ways to respond: sulk in pity or throw a party. People who respond with pity blame others and are ashamed and resentful they had to face negative circumstances. People who throw a party recognize that God helped them gain a victory so they could learn how to defeat future giants.

David clearly didn't get stuck in pity. He recognized that the battles he fought against wild animals were simply preparation for his future.

You have these same two options every time a giant comes your way. You can count it all joy that you're facing a trial, as James suggest in James 1:2, or you can sulk away in pity, distressed over what has happened.

Remember, the enemy doesn't attack what is not threatening to him. The more you step closer to God, the more you'll be a threat to the enemy—but the more you'll know personally how God can empower you to slay the giants you meet in this life.

PRAYER: Lord, thank You for setting me up to succeed in the future by giving me battles to face now. May I represent You well on the battlefield. In Jesus' name, amen.

NOTES

Step toward His empowerment.

Today's Scripture: 1 Samuel 17:38-40

When King Saul evaluated David's request to fight Goliath, he knew David would need armor and weapons. To ensure he was taken care of, Saul offered his own royal weapons—yet David refused them.

David knew he already had everything he needed: a staff, a sling, some stones, and the empowerment of heaven backing his every move.

You see, when David was taking care of his sheep, he worshipped. He magnified God and praised His power. With every song, he imprinted a picture on his own heart of how capable God was. He knew Goliath wasn't worth fearing because God was on his side.

So don't come up with your own plan to fight your giant. When giants arise, step closer to God and His Word. As you do, you'll become more confident in the fact that the extraordinary is possible because God lives on the inside of you. He will lead you to victory.

PRAYER: Lord, You are great. You are glorious. You are all I will ever need. Help me to always tune into Your power to step toward victory. In Jesus' name, amen.

NOTES

Step toward His Word.

Today's Scripture: Ephesians 6:17; Hebrews 4:12

When David approached Goliath with a shepherd's staff and a sling, Goliath was clearly unimpressed. He resorted to name-calling in order to intimidate. He didn't realize David carried a more powerful weapon that Goliath couldn't see: the Word of God.

David didn't have the Bible, but he had a relationship with God that was so deep, it overflowed to his words. Listen to the confidence that emanated from David as he talked to Goliath:

> *"Today the Lord will conquer you, and I will kill you and cut off your head. And then I will give the dead bodies of your men to the birds and wild animals, and the whole world will know that there is a God in Israel! And everyone assembled here will know that the Lord rescues his people, but not with sword and spear. This is the Lord's battle, and he will give you to us!"*
>
> **1 Samuel 17:46-47**

When facing a giant, we can operate as David did. Sharpen the weapon of God's Word through reading the Bible and prayer—then carry God's Word in our mouth. As the writer of Hebrews tells us, that Word is sharper than a two-edged sword. It is our offensive weapon for battle!

PRAYER: Lord, thank You for giving us the powerful weapon of Your Word. I commit to speaking God's Word on a regular basis. In Jesus' name, amen.

NOTES

Step toward confidence.

Today's Scripture: 1 Samuel 17:28, 33, 41-44

No one expected David to win. His brother called him prideful and full of deceit. King Saul said he was "only a boy" and Goliath himself called David a dog.

Not exactly the encouragement you need before facing a giant— particularly when the criticism comes from your family and your leader!

But David knew that their name-calling and assumptions about him weren't true. He knew who God had created him to be. In the same way, if our identity is attacked by those around us, we shouldn't listen to what they say. We should find out what God has to say about us and let that direct us.

Attacks on our identity can be mind-numbing, but they don't need to weaken our confidence in knowing God is with us, fighting for our victory.

We step closer to God every time we remember who the Bible says we are in Christ. We already have everything we need to be victorious in Him!

PRAYER: Lord, thank You that my confidence isn't in the people around me, but it is in You. Reveal to me areas where I need to change my mindset and look to You for confidence. In Jesus' name, amen.

NOTES

Step toward victory.

Today's Scripture: 1 Samuel 17:48

That first step toward Goliath may have been a little shaky. Walking toward a giant who had scared the rest of your army into silence couldn't have been easy—but it was the only way to defeat Goliath.

David's step of faith to battle Goliath was his claim to God's promises. His words meant nothing if he didn't actually go out and meet his giant face-to-face.

David put his beliefs into action.

We will face pivotal moments just as David did. If we let fear be a part of our lives, we most likely will hold back and not move toward heaven. However, if we believe God will do what He has promised, we will act on our faith. That's when we will see God's promise.

Romans 8:31 tells us, "If God is for us, who can ever be against us?" There can be peace, even in the middle of battle, when we know God's ability will always be stronger than the enemies we face.

PRAYER: Lord, thank You for constantly being by my side, even when I step out in faith. Help me to do it more often, knowing You are right there with me. In Jesus name, amen.

NOTES

SESSION 3:
HOW DO I STEP CLOSER TO GOD WHEN I'M DODGING SPEARS?

SCRIPTURE MEMORY:

Dear friends, never take revenge. Leave that to the righteous anger of God. For the Scriptures say, "I will take revenge; I will pay them back," says the Lord.

– Romans 12:19, NLT

WELCOME

Each week, give people 5-10 minutes to find your location and arrive. If possible, provide light snacks and have upbeat Christian music playing in the background until you officially begin your group meeting.

CHECKING IN

ASK: What do you value most in your relationship with people?

**WATCH: PLAY SESSION 3A OF THE
STEP CLOSER VIDEO SERIES AND
TAKE NOTES ON THE PAGE PROVIDED.**

GROUP DISCUSSION QUESTIONS

#1 READ OUT LOUD: In the video we learn that David was faced with an unprovoked attack from King Saul. By this point, David had also personally witnessed Saul's internal conflicts and toxic emotions.

>**ASK:** Why is it important for us to remain aware of the brokenness in others as David was with Saul?

#2 HAVE SOMEONE READ OUT LOUD: 1 Samuel 18:10-15

>**ASK:** What stands out to you as you read the passage?

#3 READ OUT LOUD: It's healthy to know our own weaknesses, triggers and blind spots.

>**ASK:** When and/or where are you most tempted to pick-up a figurative spear that has been thrown at you and throw it back at someone? What and/or who are the potential triggers that you might react in frustration towards?

#4 HAVE SOMEONE READ OUT LOUD: Psalm 59:1-17

>**READ OUT LOUD:** This was a psalm of David written while he was hiding from Saul.

>**ASK:** How do you see David processing his experience with God? Why was it critical that he didn't keep his hurt and anger locked up within himself?

#5 HAVE SOMEONE READ OUT LOUD: 1 Samuel 24:9-11

> **READ OUT LOUD:** : In the video, Dr. Nate referenced David's "pathway of promotion."
>
> **ASK:** What does David's example in this passage speak to you about God's pathway of promotion for your own life?

#6 ASK: Do you have any hurt or anger in your heart today that you need to process with God? Share at your own comfort level.

WORSHIP AND PRAYER TIME

PRAYER REQUESTS: Ask for everyone's prayer requests. Encourage everyone to briefly share their requests so you can spend more time praying for your requests than talking about them. Be sure to record them on the Small Group Prayer and Praise Report on pages 130-131 of this study guide. Commit to pray for each other's requests every day this week. Once all the requests are gathered, move into a group prayer time.

GROUP WORSHIP TIME:

 Before you pray for each other, invite the Presence of the Lord into your time by playing the worship video for this week (Session 3B). As the worship time concludes flow into your time of prayer by praying over the prayer requests. Encourage the group to participate by praying for one of the prayer requests that were given.

WORSHIP OPTION/ACTIVITY: If you're meeting online, in a café or in a setting that is not conducive for playing the worship video, use the following worship exercise before moving into prayer...

- Hopefully, each person selected a worshipful passage (3-5 verses) before the meeting
- Open in prayer and invite God's presence. Then have each person read back to the group their selected passage as an offering of worship.
- Once everyone has read their offering of worship, have a moment of silence (10-15 seconds) before you start to pray for each other's prayer requests.

_____

_____

_____

_____

_____

_____

_____

_____

_____

PRAYER: Take turns praying out for each others' prayer requests.

DISMISSAL

- Remind everyone about the next group meeting.
- Encourage everyone to continue to pray for each other throughout the week.
- **Worship Activity for Next Week** (If your group uses the worship activity instead of the worship videos prepare for next week in this way): Write out a personal testimony during the week for next week's meeting on page 132. This doesn't necessarily need to be a testimony of salvation, although that can be used. It could also be a testimony of miraculous answers to prayer, divine interventions or personal transformation. Write it out as a prayer of thanksgiving to God, thanking Him for each aspect of His hand at work in the situation. It could be a recent testimony or one from over a decade ago. The key is that it's a personal testimony from your life.

Choose courage.

Today's Scripture: 1 Samuel 18:5-11

Life can certainly change quickly. Everything can be going well, and then with one phone call, life feels like it's in a tailspin. Close friends turn on you. Your workplace feels hostile. Your reliable car breaks down or you face an unexpected illness.

David knows what you are going through. One minute he was working for the king; the next minute the king was throwing spears at him. David was well-liked by many people, but he was about to begin to run for his life.

Did David deserve any of this? Certainly not. Anyone of us can enter a season of dodging spears without doing anything wrong—perhaps even because we have done something right. You have to know that's okay. Some seasons your goal is to live to fight another day.

Whatever the attack is, know that God is on your side and you can handle it. It won't be easy, but as you continue to step closer to the Father, you'll find it is worth it.

PRAYER: Lord, thank You for staying close to me, even when I am under attack. I commit to stay close to You in every season of life. In Jesus' name, amen.

NOTES

Choose wisdom.

Today's Scripture: 1 Samuel 19-20

As these attacks from King Saul became more numerous, David was faced with a dilemma. Should he continue to serve in King Saul's court?

At first, the answer was yes. His good friend was Jonathan, King Saul's son. Jonathan was able to talk to his dad to find out if he truly intended to kill David. For a time, David could play the harp again without incidence. But King Saul saw the anointing on David's life and he was jealous of what God has placed on David. Ultimately, he would not rest until David was killed.

David saw this breaking point happen. He knew that he couldn't simply act as though God would take care of him if he stayed put. He had to take action to protect his life.

God wants us to use wisdom as David did. We should never blindly place ourselves in the middle of harm, and we should always stay tuned to God's direction.

Simply put: when the spears of life come, move out of the way. Run to God. Hide yourself in Him. He will protect you.

PRAYER: Lord, when I am under attack, please remind me to stop and ask You for wisdom. Help me tune my ear to hear what You have to say—and then respond. In Jesus' name, amen.

NOTES

Choose your mentors and friends.

Today's Scripture: 1 Samuel 19:11-18

Since King Saul's spears didn't kill David, Saul attempted a more direct approach. He sent troops to David's house with orders to kill him in the morning. Thanks to his wife, however, David escaped in the middle of the night.

Imagine the thoughts running through David's head as he ran away from his home. Where should he go? What should he do? He decided to run to the prophet Samuel. Then, when Saul drove him away from Samuel's, David went back to Jonathan.

When in difficulty, David ran to his spiritual mentor and to a close friend.

When you feel like you are under attack, call a mentor or connect with a godly friend. God places people in our lives for a reason: to help each other step closer to God when it is hard to step closer on our own.

This is also a good reminder to invest in the people around you... for you never know when you may be needed to help them step closer to God on their own journey!

PRAYER: Lord, thank You for giving us people who can push us toward you. Give me the courage I need to reach out and build godly relationships with those around me. In Jesus' name, amen.

NOTES

Choose your focus.

Today's Scripture: Psalm 57

When most people are under attack, they get lost in either self-pity or blame. They let their thoughts and attitudes become consumed with the momentary hurt and lose sight of the bigger purpose of life.

David's continual relationship with the Lord, however, helped him choose a different path. While he was on the run from Saul, he took time to sing. He took time to praise. He invested his thoughts in imagining God's ability and plan for his life. He wrote this from the depths of a cave while running from Saul:

"I cry out to God Most High, to God who will fulfill his purpose for me."

Psalm 57:2

When you're under attack, step back. Remind yourself that God has a plan for your life. Find a promise in the Bible that you can hold close. Journal your thoughts and see how God can encourage you in the middle of what you are facing.

The moment you're facing is difficult, but it is temporary... and God's plan for you is eternal.

PRAYER: Lord, thank You that You have a plan for my life. Even if I don't see it right now, I expect You to fulfill Your purpose for me. In Jesus' name, amen.

NOTES

Choose to vent to God.

Today's Scripture: Psalm 52:1-5; 54:3-5

Sometimes we feel boxed in by life. We want to scream, cry, and vent about how unfair life is... but we have this idea that we can't because it wouldn't be healthy or we can't complain before God.

If you read through the book of Psalms, however, you'll see that David did anything but hold back! He took his raw emotions before God and found his relief in prayer. Listen to this as he prays about the men hunting him down:

> *"...Your tongue cuts like a sharp razor; you're an expert at telling lies. You love evil more than good and lies more than truth."*

Psalm 52:2-3

David didn't vent his frustrations to the people surrounding him, but he did take them to God. He knew that time with God is the safest place to express all that is going on inside.

David also didn't leave his prayer time on a down note. He always ended in praise. "I will praise you forever, O God, for what you have done. I will trust in your good name in the presence of your faithful people" (Psalm 52:9)

Bring the good, the bad, and the ugly to God every day. He will listen.

PRAYER: Lord, I commit to being honest with You about how I feel. You know my heart so I purpose to trust You with all my frustrations. In Jesus' name, amen.

NOTES

Choose to imagine a good future.

Today's Scripture: Psalm 142

When we are in a difficult spot, our thoughts have a tendency to run away from us to disappointment and despair. We imagine what will happen if it all ends or we are harmed by the spears coming our way.

We must instead do what David did and be proactive in imagining a good future.

David wrote Psalm 142 while in a cave, hiding from King Saul. The last verse says, "Bring me out of prison so I can thank you. The godly will crowd around me, for you are good to me."

He pictured the future. He imagined the day he would become king. He saw the plan God had for him being fulfilled.

When you are at your lowest, running from spears of the enemy, take time to imagine a good future. Seasons on the run won't last forever, so picture the day you can publicly praise God, see His works in action and His plan for you fulfilled.

PRAYER: Lord, thank You that this season won't last forever. I look forward to the day when I will see Your promises proven true. In Jesus' name, amen.

NOTES

Choose to sing.

Today's Scripture: Psalm 63

Ever get a song stuck in your head and it stays with you all day long? Could that simple fact help you survive when the enemy is throwing spears at you? David seemed to think so.

When David was in a cave running from Saul, he wrote these words:

"I cry out to God Most High, to God who will fulfill his purpose for me."

Psalm 57:7-8

David understood the power of music. In fact, much of his relationship with God was probably centered around singing before the Lord.

That doesn't mean you have to be a singer to sing like David did. Just download songs from Sunday's service or play your favorite worship music and make a joyful noise before the Lord. All you need is a melody in your heart that can draw you to step closer to our Savior.

Not only will your mood improve, but as the music stays in your head, you will be continually reminded that God is with you.

PRAYER: Lord, thank You for the gift of music. I choose to sing to You during every season. In Jesus' name, amen.

NOTES

SESSION 4:
HOW DO I STEP CLOSER TO GOD WHEN MY DREAM IS GONE?

SCRIPTURE MEMORY:

And we know that God causes everything to work together for the good of those who love God and are called according to his purpose for them.

– Romans 8:28, NLT

WELCOME

Each week, give people 5-10 minutes to find your location and arrive. If possible, provide light snacks and have upbeat Christian music playing in the background until you officially begin your group meeting.

CHECKING IN

ASK: When you were a child, who did you want to grow up to be or what job did you want to do?

 **WATCH: PLAY SESSION 4A OF THE STEP CLOSER VIDEO SERIES AND TAKE NOTES ON THE PAGE PROVIDED.**

_____
_____
_____
_____
_____
_____
_____
_____
_____
_____
_____
_____
_____
_____
_____
_____
_____
_____
_____
_____
_____
_____

GROUP DISCUSSION QUESTIONS

#1 READ OUT LOUD: In the video, Jodi said, "We need to trust the Lord in the good times and the bad times."

> **ASK:** Why can it be easier for people to trust the Lord in the good times than it is to trust the Lord in the bad times?

#2 HAVE SOMEONE READ OUT LOUD: 1 Samuel 30:1-8

> **READ OUT LOUD:** There is a moment here where Ziklag is burned to the ground and David's men were discussing the possibility of stoning him to death. In this moment, David was being bombarded with thoughts of anger, discouragement and doubt about God's promises over his life as a future king.

> **ASK:** Why can it be difficult for a person to step closer to God when they feel like their dream is burned to the ground?

#3 HAVE A PERSON(S) READ OUT LOUD: 1 Samuel 30:18-20 and Romans 8:28

> **READ OUT LOUD:** In verses 18-20 of 1 Samuel 30, David experienced what God promised for all of us in Romans 8:28.

> **ASK:** Have you experienced a time when things didn't work out as planned and how did God show up in that situation?

#4 READ OUT LOUD: 1 Samuel 30:6 says that David turned and found encouragement from the Lord. In the video, Jodi mentioned different ways we can encourage ourselves in the Lord.

> **ASK:** What are some ways in which you have found encouragement in the Lord? What did that look like for you?

#5 READ OUT LOUD: God loves you so much and wants you to come to Him with everything. There is so much more in store for you... Dream, Dream, and Dream!

> **ASK:** Are there dreams you have given up on that you are willing to start dreaming about again?

WORSHIP AND PRAYER TIME

PRAYER REQUESTS: Ask for everyone's prayer requests. Encourage everyone to briefly share their requests so you can spend more time praying for your requests than talking about them. Be sure to record them on the Small Group Prayer and Praise Report on pages 130-131 of this study guide. Commit to pray for each other's requests every day this week. Once all the requests are gathered, move into a group prayer time.

GROUP WORSHIP TIME:

Before you pray for each other, invite the Presence of the Lord into your time by playing the worship video for this week (Session 4B). As the worship time concludes flow into your time of prayer by praying over the prayer requests. Encourage the group to participate by praying for one of the prayer requests that were given.

WORSHIP OPTION/ACTIVITY: If you're meeting online, in a café or in a setting that is not conducive for playing the worship video, use the following worship exercise before moving into prayer...

- Hopefully, each person wrote out a personal testimony in the form of a thanksgiving prayer to God on the next page. (or on page 132).
- Open in prayer and invite God's presence. Then have each person read back to the group their prayer of thanksgiving to the group as an offering of worship.
- Once everyone has read their offering of worship, have a moment of silence (10-15 seconds) before you start to pray for each other's prayer requests.

_____

_____

_____

_____

_____

_____

_____

_____

_____

_____

_____

_____

_____

PRAYER: Take turns praying out for each others' prayer requests.

DISMISSAL

- Remind everyone about the next group meeting.
- Encourage everyone to continue to pray for each other throughout the week.
- **Worship Activity for Next Week** (If your group uses the worship activity instead of the worship videos prepare for next week in this way): During the week, be attentive to any moment where you sense God's conviction. It could be related to an aspect God's character/ holiness or one of His purposes that He calls us to fulfill (ie caring for the poor, missions, evangelism, etc). Write it out on page 133 in preparation for week 5 in the form of a prayer. Keep it to 3-5 sentences. You can begin the prayer with, "Lord, thank You for revealing to me last week..."

Don't despair.

Today's Scripture: 1 Samuel 16:11-13; 30:1-5

David defeated a giant and then spent years running from a king who wanted to kill him... all while having a dream in his heart of becoming Israel's next king.

How far away that dream must have felt as he and the men who chose to follow him were driven from their country. And what about the day they found their home in Ziklag had been burned to the ground while they were away and their families captured?

David could still remember that moment he was anointed by Samuel, but it must have felt so distant... even impossible that he would ever become king of Israel. So David continued to trust. His dream wasn't gone; it was simply manifesting differently than expected.

So what should we do while we wait? Look at what David wrote in Psalm 37:4:

"Take delight in the Lord, and he will give you your heart's desires."

Whatever your dream is, move your trust from the dream to the Giver of your dreams. God has you and your dreams in His hand. Your journey may take longer than expected, but God's plan for you can still be fulfilled.

PRAYER: Lord, thank You for giving me a dream for my future. I choose to delight myself in You while I wait for my dream to come to pass. In Jesus' name, amen.

NOTES

Don't give up.

Today's Scripture: Psalm 34:17-22

Loss is hard.

Words can't properly describe the anguish that comes when you lose someone or something dear to you.

David and his mighty men had lost everything. Their city was burned to the ground. Everything they owned was up in smoke. Their possessions were stolen and their families were nowhere in sight.

David and his men wept.

Loss is inevitable and heartbreaking. If you have lost someone or something dear to you, take time to mourn what has happened. Take a step closer to God. Recall the last words He spoke to you. Remember His promises, including the words David wrote in Psalm 34:17-18:

> *"The Lord hears his people when they call to him for help. He rescues them from all their troubles. The Lord is close to the brokenhearted; he rescues those whose spirits are crushed."*

Let God be your source of strength when all seems lost. He will not let you down. Your story hasn't ended. It's only been interrupted.

PRAYER: Lord, I purpose to turn to You when all is lost. Thank You for being my strength when I have none. In Jesus' name, amen.

NOTES

Do encourage yourself.

Today's Scripture: 1 Samuel 30:3-6

The men who were living with David saw what God had placed inside him and they were willing to follow David as king. That's why they were living as a group in an independent state, after being driven from the country they love.

So when these mighty men came back to a burned down city and missing families, their trust in David evaporated. They were furious and ready to make David pay for what happened. They even talked of stoning him.

If you were David, what would you do? Fall on the ground and cry? Run for the hills? Draw your sword and face them?

Less than ten words describe David's next move—and these words can revolutionize your future, if you let them.

"...David found strength in the Lord his God."

Sometimes our friends can encourage us. Sometimes our pastors can encourage us, but sometimes we have no one but our own selves to lift us up.

Personal encouragement is sometimes the path out of loss.

PRAYER: Lord, I am frustrated and disappointed about what has happened, but I choose to still believe in You and Your love for me. I purpose to keep moving closer to You. In Jesus' name, amen.

NOTES

Do remember what God has done.

Today's Scripture: 1 Samuel 30:6

It's not clear what David did to strengthen himself, but more likely than not, he remembered his story. He walked through the victories God had brought him, one by one.

- David defeated lions and bears while taking care of his sheep.
- Goliath didn't stand a chance of living after taunting the Israelites as he did.
- Saul's spears could have easily taken him out, but God helped David's reflexes be strong.
- Despite desperately trying, Saul still hadn't killed David.

These are just a glimpse of the stories David had, not to mention all the countless victories he brought to the Israelite army, each of which surely had their own story of God at work.

You have stories to remember, just as David did, and every story is a significant reminder of the power God had shown you throughout your life.

If God has rescued you through each and every story up until this point, you can surely trust that He will rescue you again, even if you don't understand how He will do it.

God's power to save you and care for you hasn't changed. He is your Savior and Deliverer... and He will restore your dream.

PRAYER: Lord, thank You for reminding me of the many times you have taken care of me! I trust that I am living in a future testimony of your faithfulness. In Jesus' name, amen.

NOTES

Do reconnect with God.

Today's Scripture: Psalm 138

Not only did David sing throughout his life, but He also worshipped God. He lifted up God's name and magnified His power and loving-kindness. We know this because much of the book of Psalms is filled with the songs that David wrote.

Now when David came home to Ziklag and found out his city had been destroyed, praising God most likely wasn't his first thought. Surely he prayed through his frustration, but then turned it around and began to recount the glory, power and majesty of his Heavenly Father, Almighty God.

It's one thing to worship God when you feel like it. It's entirely another thing to worship Him when you don't feel like it, when you feel disconnected from Him, when you've lost your dream.

When you feel far from God, your personal worship of God closes that gap.

This is the most challenging time to worship—and exactly the time you will reap the most benefit from your effort. When it's the hardest thing to say, "Praise You, Lord!" and you praise Him anyway, that effort will be rewarded.

PRAYER: Lord, I feel like You are far away, but I will praise you anyway for You are my Rock and my salvation. I choose to worship regardless of how it feels. In Jesus' name, amen.

NOTES

Don't be selfish.

Today's Scripture: 1 Samuel 30:7-17

After David had encouraged himself in the Lord, he asked God if he should pursue the Amalekites. The Lord said he should. Look at what happened after they left:

> *"Along the way they found an Egyptian man in a field and brought him to David. They gave him some bread to eat and water to drink. They also gave him part of a fig cake and two clusters of raisins, for he hadn't had anything to eat or drink for three days and nights."*
>
> **-Psalm 57:7-8**

Despite the fact their families were currently in enemy territory, David and his men were not too busy for someone in need. Their desperate situation didn't deter them from taking time to help others.

It turns out that stopping to help was the best thing they could have done. When the young man was feeling better—and David promised to protect him—he led them to their enemies.

When people interrupt your plans, don't complain or ignore them. Even in our darkest times, God will give us the grace we need to put others first.

PRAYER: Lord, help me to be kind when the people around me need help. Even when my situation seems more important, I choose to value people like You value me. In Jesus' name, amen.

NOTES

Don't be stingy.

Today's Scripture: 1 Samuel 30:18-31

Although Ziklag's destruction was a loss, it wasn't a final defeat. God delivered the Amalekites into David's hand and returned everything that had been lost.

The story, however, doesn't end there. On the way back, David and 400 of his men met up with 200 of their men who had been too exhausted to continue. Some of the men who fought in the battle didn't want to share the plunder with them. They suggested the men who missed the battle could have their families, but that was it.

David wouldn't have any of this. The more he moved closer to God, the more he saw there was enough for everyone. He told his men in 1 Samuel 30:23:

"Don't be selfish with what the Lord has given us. He has kept us safe and helped us defeat the band of raiders that attacked us."

After loss, it can be easy to hold tight to what we have, even what we receive in the future. But God's plans always involve generosity. We don't need to hoard what we have been given because God is always more than enough for what we face.

PRAYER: Lord, thank You for your generous love, protection and restoration. Help me to give freely of that to others, even after terrible loss. In Jesus' name, amen.

NOTES

SESSION 5:
HOW DO I STEP CLOSER TO GOD IN THE MIDDLE OF A MESS?

SCRIPTURE MEMORY:

And he gives grace generously. As the Scriptures say, "God opposes the proud but gives grace to the humble."

– James 4:6, NLT

WELCOME

Each week, give people 5-10 minutes to find your location and arrive. If possible, provide light snacks and have upbeat Christian music playing in the background until you officially begin your group meeting.

CHECKING IN

ASK: If you could attempt anything with guaranteed success, what would it be and why?

 **WATCH: PLAY SESSION 5A OF THE STEP CLOSER VIDEO SERIES AND TAKE NOTES ON THE PAGE PROVIDED.**

GROUP DISCUSSION QUESTIONS

#1 ASK: Have you ever listened to someone who talks freely and humbly about their own mistakes? Do you find them easy to listen to and relate to? Why do you think that is?

#2 READ OUT LOUD: In the video we learned about David committing adultery with Bathsheba and the consequences from that. A mess can happen not just from adultery; but from many scenarios that can cause messes in our lives.

> **ASK:** Why is it a struggle to step closer to God in the middle of a "mess"?

#3 ASK: Have you ever created a mess where it felt hopeless and God brought you through it? How did God encourage you and surprise you as you trusted Him?

#4 ASK: How does covering up his sin make matters worse for David? How does covering up our sin from God only make things worse for us?

#5 READ OUT LOUD: In the video, Dr. Nate shared that confession means "we speak the same thing to God that He already sees in us."

> **ASK:** How does 'speaking the same thing to God that He already sees in us' free us from the deception and shame of sin?

#6 READ OUT LOUD: Psalm 51 was written by David in response to the revealing of his sin. Have someone read out loud: Psalm 51:1-19

> **ASK:** What stands out to you and what does it reveal to us about confession, repentance and mercy?

WORSHIP AND PRAYER TIME

PRAYER REQUESTS: Don't gather prayer requests at this time. Worship as a group first and then sub-group into groups of 2-3 (men with men, women with women) for prayer. In the small groups you can share how we can pray for each other.

GROUP WORSHIP TIME:

 Before you pray for each other, invite the Presence of the Lord into your time by playing the worship video for this week (Session 5B). As the worship time concludes sub-group into your smaller groups.

WORSHIP OPTION/ACTIVITY: If you're meeting online, in a café or in a setting that is not conducive for playing the worship video, use the following worship exercise before moving into prayer...

- Hopefully, each person wrote out a prayer based on a moment of conviction by the Spirit on the next page (or on page 133).
- Open in prayer and invite God's presence. Then have each person read back to the group their prayer to the group as an offering of worship.
- Once everyone has read their offering of worship, have a moment of silence (10-15 seconds).
- If you're in a café, see if it's possible to sub-group into groups of 2-3 (men with men, women with women) and share how can you pray for each other.
- If you're in an online group, consider exchanging phone numbers or emails with another person (men with men, women with women) if you feel comfortable. Share and pray with each other over the phone or via email. Engage or decline at your own comfort level and discretion.

_____

_____

_____

_____

_____

_____

_____

_____

_____

_____

_____

_____

PRAYER: Sub-group into groups of 2-3 (men with men, women with women) for prayer. Briefly share how we can pray for you in the sub-group.

DISMISSAL

- Remind everyone about the next group meeting.
- Let the group know what the plans are after the conclusion of next week's meeting. Will the group be continuing on with a new study?
- Encourage everyone to continue to pray for each other throughout the week.
- **Worship Activity for Next Week** (If your group uses the worship activity instead of the worship videos prepare for next week in this way): This week we want you to write out your own Psalm of Praise and Worship to the Lord to be read at next week's meeting. Keep it around 5-10 sentences in length. It can be simple thoughts or poetic. You can also reference the Praise and Worship vocabulary list on page 135-136 if that helps.

Avoid the thief of complacency.

Today's Scripture: 2 Samuel 11:1

The Bible does not flatter its heroes. It paints a realistic portrait of people used by God, even when they are in the middle of a mess by their own choosing. This is true of David when he was at the pinnacle of his kingdom reign. His goals had been reached, Israel was united, the borders expanded, and the country was prospering.

For some reason, he stayed home from a war. The Scripture does not detail the motivation behind his decision. Had accomplishments lulled him into self-satisfaction and a façade of fulfillment?

They certainly may have, for 1 Corinthians 10:12 warns us that in the times we feel confident and are standing strong, we should be careful not to fall. Complacency can silently sneak into our lives when we are self-assured and poised to conquer the world. At those times, we must be purposeful to continue the disciplines and spiritual routines that keep us grounded and close to God.

PRAYER: Lord, remind me that I need you just as much—if not more— in the times I feel confident and self-assured. Help me to continue moving closer to You in every season. In Jesus' name, amen.

NOTES

Avoid the thief of compromise.

Today's Scripture: 2 Samuel 11:1-4

It was a bright spring day and David had arisen from the afternoon nap he had just taken on his Jerusalem rooftop. Instead of being on the battlefield where warrior kings belong, he began to look onto a neighboring balcony where a beautiful woman was bathing. David allowed his eyes to gaze longer than they should and sinful desires began to rise.

David could have turned away. He could have left the roof in search of his favorite place to play music and begun to write a new psalm or sing one of his favorites. God, you're such a safe and powerful place to find refuge!

David could have done many other things beside the choice he made—the choice of compromise. David followed his desires and sent someone to find out who this alluring woman was and ultimately, invited her into his home.

Be careful about being in the wrong place at the wrong time. If you don't quickly turn from sinful desires, compromise is a slippery slope that will always end in disaster.

PRAYER: Lord, may I always turn to You when I want to do wrong. You are more than enough for me and can help me say no. In Jesus' name, amen.

NOTES

Avoid the thief of cover-up.

Today's Scripture: 2 Samuel 11:5-13

"I'm pregnant." Those were not the words David wanted to hear from the wife of one of his brave and committed soldiers, especially when her husband was away at war and she had just been in David's bedroom.

When you are caught in the excitement of sinful desires, potential consequences are far from your thoughts. The drinker never remembers tomorrow's hangover or the ruin of family and health. The drug user never considers that one choice as the beginning of a long, sorrowful road. The thief never considers jail and the adulterer never considers a collapsed marriage.

Instead of coming clean and confessing his sin, David attempted to cover up his affair. If only he had heeded the wisdom of son, Solomon, which was written years later:

"People who conceal their sins will not prosper, but if they confess and turn from them, they will receive mercy."

Proverbs 28:13

If you've blown it, don't cover up your sin. You can get back on track through confession and change of direction. Begin to worship God from a pure heart and you will again experience the joy of His presence.

PRAYER: Lord, thank You for your mercy. I purpose not to hide my sin, but to be open and honest before You. In Jesus' name, amen.

NOTES

Avoid the thief of conspiracy.

Today's Scripture: 2 Samuel 11:6-25

As sin often does, it leads to something worse. David invited Uriah back home under the guise of rest and relaxation, so he could be with his wife and eventually claim the baby as his own. Uriah's honor, however, kept him from doing so in a time of war. So David turned to a second plan—a conspiracy for murder. In fact, David trusted Uriah's integrity so much that he had him carry his own death sentence in a letter to the commander on the front lines of battle.

David's temptation turned to lust; lust turned into adultery. When Bathsheba's pregnancy threatened to expose his sin, he turned to deception and then murder.

What had happened to David's integrity? Is this the same man who was conscience-stricken when he cut off the corner of King Saul's robe? The mighty had certainly fallen!

Whether it is in the Garden of Eden, a rooftop, or your workplace, deception and conspiracy have always been the enemy's method of entrapment. Don't get caught in that trap; instead, come clean!

PRAYER: Lord, I choose to surrender to You, even when I've done wrong. Help me resist the devil when I am at my weakest.
In Jesus' name, amen.

NOTES

Activate the response of confession.

Today's Scripture: 2 Samuel 11:26-12:13

Are you sorry you did it or are you sorry you got caught?

It is not easy to accept responsibility for our sin. We tend to shift the blame when we find our life in the middle of a mess. Too often, we justify what we've done and pretend it's not so bad. We make excuses or blame someone else.

But David didn't. When finally confronted by his sin, he looked straight at God and told Him he messed up.

> *"Everything I did, I did right in front of you, for you saw it all. Against you, and you above all, have I sinned."*
>
> **Psalm 51:3-4 TPT**

True confession is not hiding anything from God. It is taking responsibility for our thoughts and actions and then speaking honestly before Him.

God sees your sin and knows your thoughts, motives and attitudes. Nothing is hidden from Him, so don't hold anything back. Confession empowers you to move away from sin and step back to God.

PRAYER: Lord, I'm sorry I messed up. Please forgive me and purify my heart before You. In Jesus' name, amen.

NOTES

Activate the response of cleansing.

Today's Scripture: Psalm 51:1-11

After the prophet Nathan exposed King David's adultery with Bathsheba, David composed a song confessing his wrongdoing and pleading with God for cleansing and consecration. The fear of people's opinion that drove him to cover up his sin was no longer part of his mental battle. His repentant heart is clear in Psalm 51:1-3:

> *"Everything I did, I did right in front of you, for you saw it all. Against you, and you above all, have I sinned."*

David was no longer worried about what people might think of what he had done. He wanted a clean heart before God and he poured out his appeal in this prayerful song.

The beauty and power of David's words are in his raw honesty. When we are confronted with our mistakes, may we be quick to humble ourselves before God and ask for His cleansing power to flood our soul.

David's sin was great, but God is greater. He forgives our every mistake and then empowers us to turn away from sin and step closer to Him.

PRAYER: Lord, thank You for Your cleansing grace. Make my heart new again, so I can be clean and pure and continue stepping closer to You. In Jesus' name, amen.

NOTES

Activate the response of consecration.

Today's Scripture: Psalm 51:12-19

After you confess your sin to God and are cleansed, you may still have consequences. Other people may not trust you fully or your mind may still be tempted to do wrong. Cleaning up the mess means being patient with your own self and with others as you learn how to live life differently.

David was determined to stop living deceptively, but he knew he wouldn't be able to do this on his own. That is why he asked for the Lord's help in moving forward. Thoughts of shame and guilt wouldn't stand a chance after he consecrated himself to the Lord, fully ready to turn his mess into a message.

After David consecrated his life, his passion returned. He left his messy season behind and took another step closer to God, providing us with an example of how God's mercy and forgiveness can become a reality in our lives.

When we mess up, let David's testimony of forgiveness provide a blueprint for how we can return to the Lord with all of our heart, soul, and strength.

PRAYER: Lord, thank You for giving me another chance. I purpose to tell others how You've forgiven me, so they will come back to You too. In Jesus' name, amen.

NOTES

SESSION 6:
HOW DO I STEP CLOSER TO GOD WHEN MY DREAM COMES TRUE?

SCRIPTURE MEMORY:

But that is the time to be careful! Beware that in your plenty you do not forget the Lord your God and disobey his commands, regulations, and decrees that I am giving you today.

- Deuteronomy 8:11, NLT

WELCOME

Each week, give people 5-10 minutes to find your location and arrive. If possible, provide light snacks and have upbeat Christian music playing in the background until you officially begin your group meeting.

CHECKING IN

ASK: If you had three wishes what would they be?

WATCH: PLAY SESSION 6A OF THE STEP CLOSER VIDEO SERIES AND TAKE NOTES ON THE PAGE PROVIDED.

GROUP DISCUSSION QUESTIONS

#1 READ OUT LOUD: Eventually, David's dream to become King became a reality.

>**ASK:** What are the ways that personal success can lead to spiritual dullness?

#2 HAVE SOMEONE READ OUT LOUD: 1 Chronicles 29:1-4

>**ASK:** What does this tell us about the condition of David's faith in his latter years as the king?

#3 HAVE SOMEONE READ OUT LOUD: 1 Chronicles 29:5-9

>**ASK:** As David stepped closer to God through his generosity, how did it impact those around him? How does this speak to you?

#4 HAVE SOMEONE READ OUT LOUD: 1 Chronicles 29:18-19

>**READ OUT LOUD:** David wasn't satisfied with his own dreams coming true in his life, rather, he was working on God's dreams for his son and the next generation.

>**ASK:** How does pursuing God's dream(s) for the next generation help us to step closer to God?

#5 ASK: Are there any dreams that God has given you to pursue for yourself or for others? How does the pursuit of those dreams help you to continue to step closer to God?

#6 READ OUT LOUD: Hopefully there have been multiple discoveries and moments that impacted you from this Step Closer series.

> **ASK:** Is there one discovery you've made or moment you've experienced from this series that has made a positive impact on your life? If the answer is yes, please explain.

WORSHIP AND PRAYER TIME

PRAYER REQUESTS: Ask for everyone's prayer requests. Encourage everyone to briefly share their requests so you can spend more time praying for your requests than talking about them. Be sure to record them on the Small Group Prayer and Praise Report on pages 130-131 of this study guide. Commit to pray for each other's requests every day this week. Once all the requests are gathered, move into a group worship time.

GROUP WORSHIP TIME:

Before you pray for each other, invite the Presence of the Lord into your time by playing the worship video for this week (Session 6B). As the worship time concludes flow into your time of prayer by praying over the prayer requests. Encourage the group to participate by praying for one of the prayer requests that were given.

WORSHIP OPTION/ACTIVITY: If you're meeting online, in a café or in a setting that is not conducive for playing the worship video, use the following worship exercise before moving into prayer...

- Hopefully, each person wrote out their own Psalm of Praise of Worship to the Lord (on page 134).
- Open in prayer and invite God's presence. Then have each person read back to the group their personal Psalm to the group as an offering of worship.
- Once everyone has read their offering of worship, have a moment of silence (10-15 seconds) before you start to pray for each other's prayer requests.

_____

_____

_____

_____

_____

_____

_____

_____

_____

_____

_____

_____

_____

_____

PRAYER: Take turns praying out for each other prayer requests.

DISMISSAL

- Let everyone know about what's coming up next for the group. Are you continuing with a new study next week?
- Encourage everyone to continue to pray for each other throughout the week.

Continue to dream.

Today's Scripture: 1 Chronicles 17:1

David's success finally seemed complete! He had become king, conquered armies, captured treasures, built houses, and brought back the Ark of the Covenant. But David's dreams didn't stop at his own gain and his own kingdom; he dreamed of God's glory and God's kingdom as well.

Look at the next dream in his heart:

> *"Now when David lived in his own house, David said to Nathan the prophet, "Behold, I dwell in a house of cedar, but the ark of the covenant of the Lord is under a tent."*

1 Chronicles 17:1

David didn't let success stop him from dreaming. He wanted to continue contributing to the kingdom of God, so he found new ways to serve and worship Him; he didn't get complacent.

In any area of life where we have achieved much, it's easy to sit back, relax and enjoy our success. However, we must not stop there. As long as we are still breathing, God wants to keep working through us.

PRAYER: Lord, reveal to me any areas of my heart where success has brought stagnancy. Guide me to new dreams and new challenges in your kingdom. In Jesus' name, amen.

NOTES

Continue to listen.

Today's Scripture: 1 Chronicles 22:8-10

David had the power, position and provision to build the Temple.
What he lacked was permission. The Lord had a very specific
reason why:

> *"...You have killed many men in the battles you
> have fought. And since you have shed so much
> blood in my sight, you will not be the one to build
> a Temple to honor my name. But you will have a
> son who will be a man of peace. ... He is the one
> who will build a Temple to honor my name."*

1 Chronicles 17:1

David could have put his preference before the Lord's and built the
temple anyway, but he was deliberate to follow what the Lord said.

He understood that success doesn't mean we have it all figured out.
We must keep returning to the Lord for His leading in every stage
of life.

So don't allow strength, supplies and support to supply direction.
Only prayer and time with our Lord can show us His ways... so
continue to step closer.

*PRAYER: Lord, I don't want to live by my plans alone. Guide me to
the works You have prepared for me. In Jesus' name, amen.*

NOTES

Continue to give.

Today's Scripture: 1 Samuel 29:3-4

As King of Israel, David had every right and the authority to dedicate Israel's money and supplies for the Lord's Temple. What better place to spend the treasury of the nation than on a Temple for their heavenly King?

Yet David willingly chose to give of his own personal fortune.

Freely and joyfully, David poured money into the supplies for Temple construction. His worshipping heart was developed in obscurity as a young shepherd and had only grown more generous and joyful throughout his life. Now as an old man, he opened his life once again to praise God and present his gifts.

David's reason for giving was simple: "because of my devotion to the Temple of my God" (1 Samuel 29:3).

God wants us to cultivate this same heart to give. Giving to kingdom purposes enables other people to hear direction from heaven and experience the presence of our Savior. We step closer to God any time we enable others to step closer to Him as well.

PRAYER: Lord, thank You for allowing me to be a part of Your kingdom purposes. I purpose to give of my resources to propel Your kingdom forward. In Jesus' name, amen.

NOTES

Continue to build for the future.

Today's Scripture: 1 Chronicles 22:11-16

The moment David heard that his son, Solomon, was going to build God's temple instead of him, he could have become bitter. He could have questioned God's judgment or pleaded for a different answer.

David, instead, fulfilled as much of his dream as permissible and then passed the dream on to his son. He couldn't lead the building of the temple, but he could give as much as possible to the efforts. He gave materials, generated support and gathered artists and workers. He recognized it didn't matter who accomplished the dream as long as the dream was accomplished.

David built a platform upon which his son could succeed. We need to do the same thing. Our actions at home, work, church and even in our nation, all prepare a platform from which future generations will get to grow.

So purpose to let your choices enable the next generations to reach higher in the Lord than you were ever able.

PRAYER: Lord, thank You for letting me be a part of building Your kingdom. Show me what I can do to help future generations step closer to the Lord. In Jesus' name, amen.

NOTES

Continue to inspire.

Today's Scripture: 1 Chronicles 29:3-9

As David grew in his relationship with the Lord, he detected a pattern. The people under his influence followed his lead. When he worshipped, they would worship. When he told them to attack, they did so. They trusted him.

So when it came to providing for the Temple, he wanted to use his influence well. After explaining that Solomon was building the Temple, he told the people what he did personally in the offering. Then he challenged them: "Who will follow my example and give offerings to the Lord today?" (1 Chronicles 29:5)

Look what happened next:

> *"...Then the family leaders, the leaders of the tribes of Israel, the generals and captains of the army, and the king's administrative officers all gave willingly. ... The people rejoiced over the offerings, for they had given freely and wholeheartedly to the Lord...."*

1 Chronicles 29:6, 9

His influence jumpstarted people to action. They responded because they were inspired!

You may not have influence over a nation as he did, but you do have influence among the people you know, particularly at home. So make a point to inspire people to action and cheer them on for the work of the kingdom!

PRAYER: Lord, help me act in ways that can be an example to others; give me words and actions that will inspire others to be involved in your Kingdom. In Jesus' name, amen.

NOTES

Continue to praise.

Today's Scripture: 1 Chronicles 29:10-22

After the offerings were collected, David stood before Israel and put everything in perspective.

He praised. He led the nation in praise of the greatness and glory of God. He gave people a glimpse of what He thought about Almighty God and how they could respond to God as well.

He reminded himself and everyone listening that everything they owned came from him. Their very existence was made possible because of God's love.

Then he prayed. He prayed over the Temple and the offerings given on that day. He prayed that the people would obey the Lord and continue to love Him.

The very next day David's son, Solomon, was crowned king. What a way to end that season of his life well.

David knew that without a larger perspective, we are susceptible to pride when we succeed. Praise reminds us our accomplishments are but a tiny piece of God's epic story and His vast kingdom.

PRAYER: Lord, I praise You for all that You are. All that I do comes from Your love and Your creative work in my heart and life. Thank You. In Jesus' name, amen.

NOTES

Continue to love the Lord.

Today's Scripture: Psalm 18:1-3, 20-30

Sometimes when our dreams come true, we forget those who helped us achieve them. Not so for David. David always remembered the Lord. His heart remained fixed on God to the end of his days.

He sang. He wrote psalms. He played instruments. He danced. He gave. He obeyed. He fought. He listened. He sacrificed. He humbled himself. He was teachable. He proclaimed. He repented. He sought God. He gave offerings. He prayed. He praised. In all these ways, David loved the Lord.

In triumph and failure, after he sinned and after he succeeded, David loved the Lord.

When we center our lives around a pattern of loving the Lord and stepping closer to Him in every season, we will see a satisfaction and success that is incomprehensible. It will be peace we can't understand and strength when we feel powerless, friendship when we feel lonely and joy when we have none.

Dreams will be fulfilled, loss will happen, battles will be fought and giants will fall. Through it all, the constant in our lives will be God's love and His command to step closer.

PRAYER: Lord, thank You for David's example. His love for you is still speaking generations later. May my faith truly become that steady as I step closer to You each day.

NOTES

CONCLUSION

We hope you've enjoyed the journey through *The Step Closer* experience! Our prayer is that David's secret weapon of stepping closer to God in every season will become your secret weapon as well. We also pray that your group setting will become a circle of continual encouragement and growth in your life.

Our aim and heart is that you will be empowered to...

...step closer to God when you're overlooked.

...step closer to God when you're facing a giant.

...step closer to God when you're dodging spears.

...step closer to God when your dream is gone.

...step closer to God in the middle of a mess.

...step closer to God when your dream comes true.

We sincerely believe this hidden strength will produce the kind of kingdom influence that will bring honor to Christ. We believe it will transform you from a growing disciple into an influential disciple, like David.

SMALL GROUP RESOURCES

Group Guidelines

Group Roster

Prayer & Praise Report

Worship Activities

Praise and Worship List

SMALL GROUP GUIDELINES

It's a good idea for everyone to put words to their shared values, expectations and commitments. Such guidelines will help avoid unspoken agendas and unmet expectations. We recommend you discuss your guidelines during Session One to lay the foundation for a healthy group experience. Feel free to modify anything that doesn't work for your group.

WE AGREE TO THESE VALUES:

CLEAR PURPOSE	To grow healthy spiritual lives by building a healthy small group community.
GROUP ATTENDANCE	To give priority to the group meeting (call if absent or late)
SAFE ENVIRONMENT	To create a safe place where people can be heard and feel loved (no quick answers, snap judgments or simple fixes)
BE CONFIDENTIAL	To keep anything that is shared strictly confidential within the group
CONFLICT RESOLUTION	To avoid gossip and immediately resolve concerns by following the principles of Matthew 18:15-17
SPIRITUAL HEALTH	To give group members permission to speak into my life and help me live a healthy, balanced spiritual life
LIMIT OUR FREEDOM	To limit our freedom by not serving or consuming alcohol during group activities so as to avoid causing a weaker member to stumble (1 Cor. 8:1-13; Romans 14:19-21)

WELCOME NEWCOMERS	To invite friends who might benefit from this study and warmly welcome newcomers
SCRIPTURE	While everyone's thoughts and opinions are valuable and encouraged, to ultimately rely on the truth of Scripture as our final authority
BUILDING RELATIONSHIPS	To get to know the other members of the group and pray for them regularly

SMALL GROUP ROSTER

NAME	PHONE	EMAIL

PRAYER & PRAISE REPORT

This is a place where you can write each other's requests for prayer. You can also make a note when God answers a prayer. Pray for each other's requests. If you're new to group prayer, it's okay to pray silently or to pray by using just one sentence:

"God, please help _____ to _____."

DATE	PERSON	PRAYER REQUEST	PRAISE

PRAYER & PRAISE REPORT (cont'd)

DATE	PERSON	PRAYER REQUEST	PRAISE

TESTIMONY

MOMENT OF CONVICTION BY THE SPIRIT

PSALM OF PRAISE AND WORSHIP

WORSHIP AND PRAISE LIST

Bless His Name (Psalm 103:1)

Exalt His Name (Psalm 34:3)

Glorify His Name (Psalm 96:8)

Honor His Name (Psalm 66:2)

Magnify His Name (1 Chronicles 17:24)

Praise His Name (Psalm 68:4)

"I will exalt you, my God the King; I will praise your name for ever and ever. Every day I will praise you and extol your name for ever and ever. My mouth will speak in praise of the Lord. Let every creature praise his holy name for ever and ever."
- Psalm 145:1,2,21

Praise Jesus for who He is:

Advocate - 1 John 2:1
Almighty - Rev. 1:8
Alpha & Omega (first and last)- Revelation 1:8, 22:13
Author of Life- Acts 3:15
Author & Perfector of our faith- Hebrews 12:2
Author of Salvation- Hebrews 2:10
Beloved Son - Matt. 12:18
Bright and Morning Star- Rev. 22:16
Chief Shepherd- 1 Peter 5:4
Commander of the Army of the Lord- Jos. 5:13-15
Counselor- Isaiah 9:6
Creator- John 1:3
Deliverer- Romans 11:26
Door- John 10:7,9
First & Last- Rev. 1:17
Gate- John 10:7
Glory of the Lord - Isaiah 40:5
God - Isaiah 40:3
Good Shepherd- John 10:11
Great High Priest- Hebrews 4:14
Head of the Church- Ephesians 1:22
Helper- Hebrews 13:6
Holy One- Acts 3:14
Horn of Salvation- Luke 1:69
The Just- Acts 3:14
I Am- John 8:58
Image of God- 2 Corinthians 4:4
Immanuel- Isaiah 26:4
King- Zechariah 9:9
King Eternal- 1 Timothy 1:17
King of Kings- 1 Timothy 6:15
King of the Ages- Revelation 15:3
Lamb- Revelation 13:8
Lamb of God- John 1:29
Leader- Isaiah 55:4

Life- John 14:6
Light of the World- John 8:12
Lord of All- Acts 10:38
Lord of Glory- 1 Corinthians 2:8
Lord of Lords- 1 Timothy 6:15
Lord of Righteousness- Jerimiah 23:6
Mediator- 1 Timothy 6:15
Messiah- Daniel 9:25
Mighty God- Isaiah 9:6
Only Begotten Son- John 1:18
Our Passover- 1 Corinthians 5:7
Prince of Peace- Acts 3:15
Prophet- Luke 24:19
Redeemer- Proverbs 23:11
Righteous One- Acts 7:52
Resurrection & Life- John 11:25
Rock- 1 Corinthians 10:4
Rose of Sharon- Song of Solomon 2:1
Ruler- Matthew 2:6
Savior- Luke 2:11
Song of God- Matthew 2:15
Son of the Most High- Luke 1:32
Sun of Righteousness- Malachi 4:2
True Light- John 1:9
True Vine- John15:1
Truth- John 1:14
Word of Life- John 1:1
Word of God- Revelation 19:3
Wonderful- Isaiah 9:6
Bless His Name (Psalm 103:1)
Exalt His Name (Psalm 34:3)
Glorify His Name (Psalm 96:8)
Honor His Name (Psalm 66:2)
Magnify His Name (1 Chronicles 17:24)
Praise His Name (Psalm 68:4)

Praise God for who He is:

Almighty- Genesis 17:1
Benevolent- Psalm 145:9,15,16
Eternal God- Deuteronomy 33:27
Fortress- 2 Samuel 22:2
Good- Psalm 145:7
Gracious- Exodus 34:6
Healer- Exodus 15:26; Psalm 107:20
Heavenly Father- Matthew 6:26
Holy- Psalm 22:3
The "I AM"- Exodus 3:14
Immutable (never changes)- Malachi 3:6
Jehovah- Exodus 6:3
Judge- Genesis 18:25
Just- Zephaniah 3:5
Living God- Joshua 3:10
Lord Almighty- 1 Samuel 1:11
Lord God- 1 Chronicles 29:10; Matthew 6:9
Lord of Lords- Deuteronomy 10:17
Loving- 1 John 4:8
Loving kindness- Psalm 144:2
Merciful- Psalm 145:8
Most High- Deuteronomy 32:8
Our Strength- Exodus 15:2
Omnipotent (all powerful)- Job 42:2
Omnipresent- Psalm 139:7-12
Omniscient- Psalm 147:5
Peace- Judges 6:24
Provider- Genesis 22:14
Refuge- Psalm 144:2
Righteous- Jerimiah 23:6
Shield- Psalm 144:2

Praise the Holy Spirit for who He is. Ask him to magnify his work in you. His works include:

Counselor- John 14:6
Power of the Highest- Luke 1:35
Spirit of Adoption- Romans 8:15
Spirit of Counsel- Isaiah 11:2
Spirit of Fear (of the Lord)- Isaiah 11:2
Spirit of Grace- Zechariah
Spirit of Holiness- Romans 1:4
Spirit of Knowledge- Isaiah 11:2
Spirit of Prophecy- Revelation 19:10
Spirit of Understanding- Isaiah 11:2
Spirit of Wisdom- Isaiah 11:2

Made in the USA
Columbia, SC
29 August 2018